D0102985

# DIFFICULT RIDDLES
# FOR SMART KIDS 2

## ANOTHER 300 RIDDLES & BRAIN TEASERS
## THAT KIDS AND FAMILIES WILL LOVE

### M. PREFONTAINE

M. Prefontaine has asserted his moral right to be identified as the author of this work in accordance with the Copyright, Designs and Patents Act 1988.

All rights reserved. No part of this publication may be reproduced, stored in a retrieval system, or transmitted in any form or by any means, electronic, mechanical, photocopying or otherwise without the prior permission of the copyright owner.

Published by MP Publishing

Copyright © 2019

## Other Children's books by the author
### (selection)

**Difficult Riddles for Smart Kids**

**Math Riddles for Smart Kids**

**Riddles for Kids: Over 300 Riddles and Jokes for Children**

**Jokes for Kids**

**Best Jokes Book for Kids: Over 900 Jokes, Riddles, Tongue Twisters, Knock Knock Jokes and Limericks that Children will Love**

**Tongue Twisters for Kids: Over 150 of the Toughest Tongue Twisters that Children will Love**

**Knock Knock Jokes for Kids: A Joke Book for Children**

# CONTENTS

# INTRODUCTION

*"The mind once stretched by a new idea, never returns to its original dimensions."*

*Ralph Waldo Emerson*

This is a sequel to the best-selling riddles book *Difficult Riddles for Smart Kids*, and is written to provide even more entertainment for children and families.

It's a collection of another 300 brain teasing riddles and puzzles that are not meant to be easy but to encourage problem solving and lateral thinking. The book also empowers children to befuddle their families and friends with perplexing riddles and is ideal for long journeys.

The riddles are laid out in three chapters which get more difficult as you go through the book, in the author's opinion at least. The answers are at the back of the book if all else fails.

Enjoy!

# DIFFICULT RIDDLES

1. You draw a line. Without touching it, how do you make the line longer?

2. What is it that you can give away but still have it for yourself?

3. A boy fell off a 20-foot ladder but did not get hurt. Why not?

4. What is the first thing you see in an emergency that is also something you only see twice in a lifetime?

5. I am as simple as a circle, worthless as a leader, but when I follow a group, their strength increases tenfold. By myself, I'm practically nothing. What am I?

6. What word when pronounced wrong is right, but when pronounced right is wrong?

7. What flies all day but never goes anywhere?

8. What sort of stones will you never find in the ocean?

9. I have a 100-foot piece of string. It takes me two seconds to cut a one-foot length. How long will it take me to cut the string into 100 one-foot lengths?

10. What is the most curious letter?

11. What is always freezing but never wears a coat?

12. What will an empty hand fill?

13. What can get broken without being touched?

14. What kind of nuts are the softest?

15. If a dozen eggs cost 12 cents how much do 100 eggs cost?

16. How many birthdays does the average person have?

17. A half is a third of what?

18. All men take their hats off to one person. Who is this esteemed person?

19. I am a fruit with seeds on the outside. What am I?

20. Every country has one, though they are different. They wave to their citizens, throughout the wind and rain. What are they?

21. Some months have 30 days, some months have 31 days; how many have 28?

22. I am the only fruit or vegetable that is never sold canned, frozen or processed in any way other than fresh. What am I?

23. I am the kind of soda you must not drink. What am I?

24. What turns everything around without moving?

25. Why is the math book sad?

26. I can go up and down at the same time heading towards the clouds and the ground. What am I?

27. What can you put through glass without shattering it?

28. Who gets paid when they drive away their customers?

29. A friend was telling me that he has eight sons and each brother has a sister. In total, how many children does my friend have?

30. What driver never gets arrested?

31. What has two legs but doesn't walk, but can climb?

32. What type of paper can you neither read nor write on?

33. I can run but have no feet. I can roar but have no mouth. I wear a belt but have no waist. I need to drink but never eat. What am I?

34. What nut has a hole in the middle and is squishy?

35. Which button has no function despite being pressed?

36. I have a thousand wheels but don't move. People say I am a lot, but I am just one. What am I?

37. What is it that has a bottom at the top of them?

38. What has four fingers and a thumb but is not alive?

39. What is higher without a head on it?

40. First, think of the color of the clouds. Next, think of the color of snow. Now, think of the color of a bright full moon. Now answer quickly what do cows drink?

41. What body part is pronounced as one letter but is written with three, only two letters are used?

42. You are sat on a horse. In front of you is a car and behind you is an airplane. Where are you?

43. What has a foot but no leg?

44. I can be as thin as a picture frame but through my insides I can show you the world. What am I?

45. What happens when you throw a blue rock into the yellow sea?

46. How is it that all your cousins can have an aunt who isn't your aunt?

47. What kind of tree is carried in your hand?

48. What jumps higher than any building?

49. What is always in front of you and can never be behind you?

50. I can run but can't walk and wherever I go thoughts follow close behind. What am I?

51. A girl goes to a shop and buys one dozen eggs. As she is going home, all but three break. How many eggs are left unbroken?

52. What can you blow up that stays intact?

53. I can move from there to here by disappearing, and here to there by reappearing. What am I?

54. What has a head and a tail but no body?

55. What is it that falls down but never gets hurt?

56. You are given two candles of equal size, which can burn 1 hour each. You have to measure 90 minutes with these candles. How do you do it only using the candles and a match?

57. What is it that is always behind time?

58. There are two ducks in front of a duck, two ducks behind a duck and a duck in the middle. What is the minimum number of ducks in total?

59. What is often returned but cannot be borrowed?

60. I was at my Aunt's house admiring myself in the mirror. In the mirror I saw the reflection of her analogue clock behind me. The reflected time said 2.30. What time was it really?

61. James' and Alex's last names were Smith and Jones, but not necessarily in that order. Two of the following statements are false.
James' last name is Smith
James' last name is Jones
Alex's last name is Smith
What are their real names?

62. You are in a boat about a mile from shore when someone shoots a rifle in your direction from shore. You hear the shot, see it hit the water and see the smoke from the rifle.
Which would make you first aware of the shot?

63. Ian was born on Christmas Day but his birthday is in the summer. How is this?

64. What can you hold without ever touching or using your hands?

65. If you reverse the order of the numbers in my age you will get double my age next year. How old am I?

66. I have put a collection of three different colored marbles into a bag. How many would you need to take out to be certain of having two of the same color?

67. Why do Chinese men eat more rice than Japanese men?

68. A book slipped from a man's hands in the library and fell on the floor with a loud noise. 20 eyes looked at him. How many people were in the library?

69. What do you call someone with a nose but no body?

70. I climb higher as I get hotter. I can never escape from my crystal cage. What am I?

71. I have a ring but no fingers. I used to stay still all the time but nowadays I follow you around. What am I?

72. I have rings but they are not of any great value. I would be given on a fifth wedding anniversary. What am I?

73. You have two dogs. How can you give one away, yet keep both?

74. Three doctors said that Jack was their brother. Jack said he had no brothers. Who is lying?

75. Sophie's father is Roy. Then Roy is the _____ of Sophie's father?

76. A girl and a boy each have a bag containing the same number of marbles. How many marbles must the boy give the girl so that she has twenty more than him?

77. Jack and Bill were playing a game of tennis. To make it interesting they decided to bet $1 on each game. Jack won five bets and Bill won $7 when they had finished. How many games did they play?

78. What is easy to lift but difficult to throw?

79. Which letter comes next in the sequence: S, M, H, D, W, M, ?

80. A harp has four while a violin and a guitar each have six. What am I referring to?

81. How is Europe like a frying pan?

82. Which is greater: six dozen dozens or half a dozen dozens?

83. Today is a Friday. What day of the week is it 5,500 days from today?

84. What does Brazil produce that no other country produces?

85. I am a word that begins with the letter 'e' but have only one letter within me. What am I?

86. I have got three eyes which are in a straight line. I have a red eye which when it opens freezes everything. What am I?

87. What jumps when it walks and sits when it stands?

88. What takes a bow before it speaks?

89. I can be metal or bone and have many teeth, though my bite hurts no one. What am I?

90. I am not an airplane, but I can fly through the skies. I am not a river but I can still drown people. What am I?

91. It takes one word to separate them, otherwise they are inseparable. What are they?

92. What is the difference between yesterday and tomorrow?

93. What kind of dog never bites?

94. I can shave every day, but my beard will stay the same. Who am I?

95. A is the sister of B. B is the brother of C. C is the father of D. How is D related to A?

96. There has been a heavy snowfall. James gets twice as much snow in his garden as Kate does. Why is this?

97. I am white and round, but not always around. Sometimes you see me and sometimes you don't. What am I?

98. It does not matter how much older a sibling is, eventually a younger sibling will be half as old as the older one.
Is this statement always true?

99. I am so simple that I can only point, but I can guide people all over the world. What am I?

100. I have a tongue but never talk. I have no legs but often walk. What am I?

101. Your mother's brother's only brother-in-law is asleep on your couch. Who is asleep on your couch?

102. What bee flies around the garden but can be handled without a sting?

103. What speaks every language in the world?

104. I have feathers to help me fly. I have a body and head, but I'm not alive. It is your strength which determines how far I go. You can hold me in your hand, but I'm never thrown. What am I?

105. I can fill a room completely but take up no space. What am I?

106. What is the shortest complete sentence in the English language?

107. When I am by myself, I am 24th. If there are two of me, I am 20. What am I?

108. Two large sacks, one moment nearly empty, the next full to the brim, the contents more valuable than diamonds. Can be filled up with water but you wouldn't want that. What are we?

109. You're a bus driver. At the first stop 4 people get on. At the second stop 8 people get on; at the third stop 2 people get off and, at the fourth stop, everyone gets off. The question is what color are the bus driver's eyes?

110. What remains in the same place even when it goes off?

111. When will a net hold water?

112. I can be an end to all words but never make a sound. What am I?

113. I am a fruit, but you can also find me in a calendar. What am I?

114. A doctor's son's father is not a doctor. How is this?

115. There were two boys who wanted to cross a river. They could only do this by boat. However, the boat was not very big and could only take one boy at a time. They have no ropes and the boat won't return on its own. How did they both manage to get across the river?

116. I am a king whose measures are always right. What am I?

117. The first time you have me I am free as I am the second time also. However, the third time you have me will cost you money. What am I?

118. One fourth of the population of a newly discovered planet have 4 legs. The rest have 2 legs. There are 60 legs in total. How big is the population of the newly discovered planet?

119. A group of soldiers were on parade and facing due west. Their sergeant shouted at them; right turn, about turn and left turn. Which direction are they now facing?

120. What was the last year that read the same upside down as right way up?

121. A wise king devised a contest to see who would receive the princess' hand in marriage. The princess was put in a 50×50 foot carpeted room. Each of her four suitors was put in one corner of the room with a small box to stand on. The first one to touch the princess' hand would be the winner and become the new king. The rules of the test were that the contestants could not walk over the carpet, cross the carpet, or hang from anything; nor could they use anything but their body and wits. One suitor figured out a way and married the princess and became the new king. What did he do?

122. I am a stone in wood which will help put your thoughts into words, but as I do the smaller I get. What am I?

123. A duck was given $9, a spider was given $36 and a bee $27. How much did the cat receive?

124. What has the number seven two of that the rest of the numbers between one and ten have only one of?

125. What grows up and grows down at the same time?

126. What's the difference between a well-dressed man on a bicycle and a poorly-dressed man on a tricycle?

127. A chain is nailed to a wall. The chain is 10 foot long and the two ends are hung on the wall. The chain dips by 5 foot from either end. How far apart are the two ends?

128. You can easily see me but not touch me. You can put me out, but you still have me. What am I?

129. There was an engineer and a lawyer waiting in line for the movies. One was the father of the other one's son. How was this?

130. I saw an unusual book. The foreword comes after the epilogue, the end is in the first half of the book and the index comes before the introduction. What is the book?

131. I am a band but don't perform or sing but can keep groups together. What am I?

132. Which word is the odd one out: First, Second, Third, Forth, Fifth, Sixth, Seventh, and Eighth?

133. What do cinders, charcoal, embers and fire have that smoke simply doesn't have?

134. In which situation do you start at red and stop at green?

135. This turns into a different story. What is it?

136. A person who is mute goes into a shop to buy a toothbrush. He imitates brushing his teeth to the assistant and successfully purchases a toothbrush. Next a blind person goes into the shop to buy a comb. How does he indicate what he wants to the assistant?

137. I am a sister, but I may not have any siblings. Who am I?

138. Two brothers live on either side of a bridge. They can see everything but each other. Who are they?

139. What gets very hot but never sweats, and has a door which you can't go through?

140. What can you find here, there and everywhere?

141. I wasn't telling the truth when I denied arguing against scrapping the proposal. Was I in favor of or against the proposal?

142. "Everything I tell you is a lie," am I telling you the truth or a lie?

143. You are driving your car at 80 mph. You can only drive on the road as it is a narrow road and on one side there is a mountain and on the other side there is a deep valley. A car is heading towards you on the right side of the road and an old man is walking on the left side of the road. What do you decide to hit to minimize the damage?

144. Justin says to his sister Sarah, "because I'm twice as old as you, I'm twice as smart, too." His sister responds, "yes, but in five years I'll be twice as old as I am now, and you won't." How old will Sarah and Justin be in five years?

145. Which American city is 3/7 chicken, 2/3 cat and 1/2 goat??

146. After a party a man has 21 bottles of wine. A total of seven of the bottles are full, seven are half full and seven are empty. The man wants to divide the bottles to his three guests so that they each have the same number of full bottles, half full bottles and empty bottles to take home. How does he manage to do it?

147. What can go through a door but never goes in or out of the room?

148. Four friends are going to a basketball game and there are just five seats left. How many different combinations can four people sit in five seats?

149. Which of the following words doesn't belong in the group and why?
CORSET, COSTER, SECTOR, ESCORT, COURTS?

150. An Indian emperor has an elephant that he wants to ship to his friend further along the coast. His friend asks how heavy it is. Unfortunately, the emperor's scales will only weigh up to 50 lbs. How can he discover the elephant's weight?

151. A man bought a beautiful horse and needed a paddock to keep it in. He decided on a square shaped area and used 30 poles on each side of the square. How many poles did he use?

152. A man was busy at work and phoned his wife and asked her to pick some things up for him on her shopping trip. He said there was an envelope on his desk and the amount of money was written on the outside. She found it and it had 98 written on it. However, when she bought $ 90 of goods, she didn't have $ 8 left over but was $ 4 short. Why was this?

153. In which sport do the winners move backwards and the losers move forward?

154. There are four snails in a race - Tom, Paul, Laura, and Ester. In what order did the snails cross the finish line if
A) Laura finished four hours ahead of Ester.
B) Paul crawled across the finish line eight hours before Tom.
C) Tom needed six hours longer to finish the course than Laura did.

155. No matter how much or how little you use me you will change me once a month. What am I?

156. Can you make the numbers
1,2,3,4,5,6,7,8 and 9
add up to 100? You can use addition, subtraction, division and multiplication but the numbers must stay in the same order.

157. I have one and a person has two, a citizen has three and a human being has four, a personality has five and an inhabitant of earth has six. What am I?

158. There were seven brothers who were all born exactly 2 years apart. The youngest brother is seven years old. How old is the oldest brother?

159. In a small Canadian town, all the residents speak either English, French or both. 80% of the people speak English and 40% speak French. How many speak both languages?

160. I can dance but have no legs. I can breathe but have no lungs. I can live and die, but have no life. What am I?

161. If 5 cats can catch 5 mice in 5 minutes, how many cats do you need to catch 100 mice in 100 minutes?

162. You intercepted this coded message sent by an enemy operative:
YYURYYUBICURYY4ME
What does it mean?

163. A man is 90 centimeters plus half his height tall. How tall is he?

164. A brick is put on a set of scales. It evenly balances with ¾ of a pound and ¾ of a brick. What is the weight of a whole brick?

165. I am a five-letter word. If you remove my first letter, I will still sound the same. Remove my last letter and I still sound the same. Even remove my letter in the middle, I will still sound the same. What am I?

166. There is a pair of twin sisters and they are different in one respect. One of the girls will always tell the truth and the other one will always lie. What one yes/no question could you ask to either one of the sisters to figure out which one is lying?

167. A smart coconut seller has a long way to go to take his coconuts to the market. He has to go through 30 checkpoints on the way and at each checkpoint he has to pay a tax of one coconut for every sack of coconuts he is carrying. On this trip he is taking 3 sacks which each have 30 coconuts in them. What is the maximum number of coconuts that he can have with him when he gets to the market?

168. What has a constant speed but doesn't go anywhere?

169. What can pass before the sun but never has a shadow?

170. A mother has five children. Four of their names are Michael, Tania, William and Theresa. Is the fifth child's name Frank, Anna, Sally or Michelle?

171. Assume you have a pile of pennies as high as the Empire State building, which is 443 meters high. Could you fit this pile of pennies into a cube measuring 1 meter x 1 meter x 1 meter high?

172. A train travels without stopping from A to B at a constant speed of 60 mph. Another train travels from B to A without stopping at a constant speed of 40 mph. How far apart will they be an hour before they cross?

173. A train, which is a mile long, is moving at 60 mph when it reaches a mile-long tunnel. How long does it take for the entire train to pass through the tunnel?

174. Nearly everyone sees me but doesn't notice me because they are more interested in what is behind me. What am I?

175. I am only stones and metal but am held above kings. What am I?

176. A man and his dog are on opposite sides of a river. The man calls to his dog and he comes to him without getting wet or using a boat or bridge. How did the dog manage this?

177. I can be long or short. I can be grown or bought. I can be painted or left bare. I can be round or square. What am I?

178. The police are investigating an oil smuggling syndicate and are on the trail of the boss. They receive a message from an informant which says:
710 57735 34 5508 51 7718
Is the boss' name Bill, Jack or Simon?

179. What can be driven but doesn't have any wheels, and can be sliced yet remains whole?

180. Jack's father is three times his age. In eleven years, Jack will be half his father's age. How old are Jack and his father today?

181. What five everyday items will you find in 'a tennis court'?

182. I feed upon swords, spades and rakes. I can pierce armor that none can break. One drop and I can stop a watch, but without time I will not grow. What am I?

183. What question can you ask all day and get different, but correct, answers?

184. It's shorter than the rest but when you are happy you raise it above the others. What is it?

185. I can fly without wings and catch my food with a silver rope. What am I?

186. I have a brother and we both run for thousands of miles but can never meet. What am I?

187. I have thousands of ribs but only two backbones. What am I?

188. The Pacific Ocean is in which state?

189. In the spring I put my clothes on, and as it warms up the more clothing I wear. As the cold weather comes, I discard all my clothes. What am I?

190. Of the king I am blue and of the peasant I am red. Of the toad I am cold but of the dog I am hot. What am I?

191. What breaks on water but never on land?

192. What rotates but doesn't move, will heat but doesn't get hot and doesn't have arms but waves?

193. Take away my first letter, then my second letter. Then take away all my letters and I remain the same. What am I?

194. I am a God, a planet and can measure heat. What am I?

195. I have no legs, but I can run to work. I have no money, but I can still charge. What am I?

196. A gambler is given a choice of bets. He can double his money if he can do one of the following:
A) Roll 1 die and get a 4 or above.
B) Roll 2 dice and get a 5 or 6 on at least one of them.
C) Roll 3 dice and get a 6 on at least one die.
Which bet, if any, should he take?

197. If you put a roast in a roaster what do you put in a toaster?

198. What do you make by sitting down, or by running for 400 meters, and even a cat can do by drinking milk?

199. A donkey travels the exact same distance daily. Strangely, 2 of his legs travel 40 kilometers and the remaining two travel 41 kilometers. Obviously, two donkey legs cannot be 1 km ahead of the other two. The donkey is perfectly normal. So how can this be true?

200. How many 'F's are there in the following sentence?
Finished files are the result of years of scientific study combined with years of experience.

201. What has six faces but never wears makeup and has twenty-one eyes but still cannot see?

202. A man bought two cars. However, he decided that neither car was suitable for him and sold them for $ 6000 each. He made a 20% profit on one of them and a 20% loss on the other. How much profit or loss did he make on these two cars?

203. A man and a dog were going down the street. The man rode a horse yet walked. What was the dog's name?

204. What can be measured and keeps moving forward but is not seen?

205. You have three boxes A, B, and C. Inside each box is a colored marble. One marble is red, one is white, and one is blue. You do not know which marble is in which box. Then, you are told that of the next three statements only one is true:
Box A contains the red marble.
Box B does not contain the red marble.
Box C does not contain the blue marble.
Which color marble is in which box?

206. You go in through one hole, you come out through three holes. Once you're inside you're ready to go outside, but once you're outside you're still inside. What is it?

207. I am nothing more than holes tied to each other but can be as strong as steel. What am I?

208. I can be used to bat with, but I never get hit. I am near a ball which is never thrown. What am I?

209. It takes a total of 10 minutes to fry a steak – 5 minutes for each side. The pan that you are using can only hold two steaks. What is the shortest period of time that you can cook 3 steaks in?

210. I have a thousand needles but cannot sew. What am I?

211. What is used to greet people and also to describe something taller than you?

212. What is drawn by everyone without pen or paper?

213. A man and a woman are going home by car. They are stopped by a policeman and he asks how they are related. The man answers:
"Her father-in-law is my father-in-law's father."
How are they related?

214. Seven brothers of whom five work all day. The other two just work or play. Who are the brothers?

215. I am found in the sea and on land, but I do not walk or swim. I travel by foot, but I am toeless. No matter where I go, I'm never far from home. What am I?

216. What flies when it is born, lies with its siblings while it is alive but will run away once it is dead?

217. What is the shortest English sentence which contains all the letters of the alphabet?

218. I come to you shattered and broken. Though I will not say a word I will reveal to you a new world if you have the patience to mend me. What am I?

219. If I don't keep time correctly, I can result in death. I give a beating which doesn't hurt but helps give life. What am I?

220. A house of wood which is built in a hidden place. Built without nails or glue and high above the earthen ground. It holds gems of many colors. What is it?

221. What does an Island and the letter T have in common?

222. In what language can four be half of five?

223. There are many different types to choose but the one you pick is always no good. What is it?

224. What has no mouth but still whistles and has two 't's but will make many more?

225. I can move forwards and backwards but don't have legs. I cannot talk, I cannot walk, I don't slither or crawl across the floor either. I come in different shapes, sizes and colors. What am I?

226. The six words below each have the same highly unusual feature. What is it?
Almost, begin, below, empty, first, glory

227. Jack is younger than Rodney but older than Debbie. Larry is older than Sophie who is older than Jack. Rodney is older than Larry. Who is the middle child?

228. I have many faces, expressions and emotions. I can be found with a simple tap. What am I?

229. What is unusual about the following words: revive, banana, grammar, voodoo, assess, potato, dresser, uneven?

230. If I had one more sister I would have twice as many sisters as brothers. If I had one more brother, I would have the same number of each. How many brothers and sisters do I have?

231. I cannot be burned in fire nor drowned in water. What am I?

232. There is a one-mile bridge which can only carry a 25-ton truck on it or it will break. Fred is driving his lumber truck which weighs exactly 25 tons before it enters the bridge.
When Fred is three quarters of the way across the bridge a small bird lands on his truck. However, it doesn't break the bridge. Why is that?

233. Jack never tells a lie. He is asked to think of one number from 1,2 or 3.
You must ask Jack one question, the answer for which is yes or no or don't know, which will reveal the number Jack is thinking of. What question would you ask?

234. I can be thin but not fat, in your body but not on the menu. I am better when I am fresh, but you will never see me. What am I?

235. Three of the four words are given in code. The codes are not arranged in the same order as the words and one code is missing. When you have cracked the code, use it to find the code for the word steel:
TEAM      MALE      MAST      LEST
6245      5326      1345

236. There are 12 children in a classroom. 6 children are wearing socks and 4 are wearing shoes. 3 children are wearing both. How many have bare feet?

237. A man lights two candles of equal length while he eats dinner, however one candle is thicker than the other. The thick candle is designed to last for 6 hours while the thin candle is designed to last for 3 hours.
At the end of the dinner, the thick candle is twice as long as the thin candle. How long did the dinner last?

238. The police are investigating a murder and there are five suspects, one of whom is the guilty party. Each of the suspects gives one statement and it later transpires that just three of these statements are correct.
These are the statements:
Uncle Jack: "Uncle Jim committed the murder."
Aunt Mary: "I did not do it."
Cousin Stewart: "It was not Cousin Margaret."
Uncle Jim: "Uncle Jack is lying when he says I did it."
Cousin Margaret: "Aunt Mary is telling the truth."
Who committed the murder?

239. Some alphas are betas.
All betas are gammas.
Some gammas are deltas.
Some deltas are betas.
Therefore, some alphas are definitely deltas.
Is the above conclusion true or false?

240. Alex bought a bag of apples on Saturday and ate a third of them. On Sunday, he ate half of the remaining apples. He ate one on Monday, one on Tuesday, and then ate half of the remaining apples on Wednesday. On Thursday he looked in the bag and saw that there was just one apple left. How many apples did the bag have to begin with?

241. At a school there are 100 students. A total of 55 play basketball, 44 play baseball and 20 play both. How many play neither?

242. John is looking at Betty, but Betty is looking at Bill. John is married, but Bill is not. Is a married person looking at an unmarried person?
A) Yes
B) No
C) Cannot be determined

243. If you have 3, then you have 3. If you have 2, then you have 2. But if you have 1, then you have none. What is it?

244. Sara is Bill's niece, but she's not Julie's niece, even though Julie is Bill's sister and Bill isn't married. How is Sara related to Julie?

245. We have to determine a 3-digit number and are given 5 clues. They are:
A) 682 – One number is correct and correctly positioned
B) 614 – One number is correct but incorrectly positioned
C) 206 – Two numbers are correct but both incorrectly positioned
D) 738 – None of the numbers are correct
E) 780 – One number is correct but incorrectly positioned
What is the number?

246. They are three erors in this question. Can you spot them?

247. I point without fingers, I strike without arms and run without feet. What am I?

248. What 10 letter English word can be typed using only the top row of a standard keyboard?

249. I am a home without doors. I have only one occupant during my life and am useless once they leave. What am I?

250. Thousands make gold within this house. It is guarded by countless spears but a sweet reward for the brave. What am I?

251. I work when I play and play when I work. What am I?

252. What is the only letter of the alphabet that doesn't appear on the periodic table?

253. What are moving left to right at this very moment?

254. When does water stop going downhill?

255. I am always in you and sometimes on you. If I surround you, I can kill you. What am I?

256. I make two people out of one. What am I?

257. In a race Bill is the fiftieth fastest and the fiftieth slowest runner. Assuming no runners are running at the same speed how many runners are there in the race?

258. I am powerful but have no life. Despite that I can still die. What am I?

259. What two whole positive numbers make a single digit when multiplied together and two digits when added?

260. When I point up everything is bright, but when I point downwards it is dark. What am I?

261. What are the next three letters in the series: WATNTL

262. You have a valuable ring which you want to post to a friend. You also have a strong box with a lock. However, while you have a key, your friend doesn't. How can you give your ring securely to your friend through the post?

263. An apple tree has apples on it. A strong wind blows through the area and there are no longer apples on the tree. However, there also aren't apples on the floor. How is this the case?

264. What is the odd word out in the following list?
Flow, snip, trap, draw, back

265. There are four boxes and each has a different colored ball in it. People are then asked to guess which colored ball is in which box.
In total 150 people participate in the contest.
When the boxes are opened, it turns out that 66 people have guessed none of the balls correctly, 42 people have guessed one ball correctly, and 28 people have guessed two balls correctly.
How many people have guessed three balls correctly, and how many people have guessed four balls correctly?

266. Turn us on our backs, open up our stomachs, and devour our contents and you will be among the wisest of men. What are we?

267. What is the probability that during your lifetime you will meet someone with more than the average number of legs?

268. A King and Queen were having afternoon tea together. They asked for iced tea. However, the Queen drank much faster and had five teas while the King only had one. It turns out the tea was poisoned, and the King died, though the Queen was unaffected. Why did the King die even though he drank less tea than the Queen?

269. A cheetah saw 6 elephants while going towards the river. Each elephant saw 2 monkeys going towards the river. Each monkey has one parrot in their hands. How many animals are going towards the river?

270. A prince wished to marry a beautiful princess. However, the wise King said he could only have his daughter's hand if he could solve a puzzle.
He said that there were 27 scorpions and 4 cages to put them in. He must put the scorpions into the 4 cages so that there were an odd number in each cage.
The prince married the princess. How did he manage it?

271. Jack is sent off to the market by his father with the instruction that he has to buy 100 eggs and he gives him 100 cents. When he gets to the market, he finds that there are only three types of eggs. They are:
20 goose eggs cost 1 cent.
1 chicken egg costs 5 cents
1 duck egg costs 1 cent.
What combination of eggs must he buy to exactly spend 100 cents on 100 eggs?

272. You have a cold and go and see the doctor. He gives you four tablets, two to stop you coughing and two for your fever. You have to take one of each for the next two days. However, the tablets all look the same and the doctor put them all in the same packet. How do you follow the doctor's instructions and take one of each type of tablet for the next two days?

273. Harry has trouble remembering his 5-digit PIN but is good at problem solving. So, in order to remember it he set himself clues to the number. These are:

A) The fourth digit is four greater than the second digit.

B) There are three pairs of digits that each sum to 11.

C) The third of the five digits is three less than the second.

D) The first digit is three times the fifth digit.

What is Harry's 5-digit PIN?

274. A man bought a one-foot tree from his garden center which he was told was very fast growing. On the first day it increased its height by a half, on the second day it grew by a third and on the third day by another quarter and so on. How long did the tree take to grow to one hundred feet?

275. Sara went for a picnic with her friends Becky and Carly. Becky brought three cakes to the picnic and Carly brought five. All the cakes were the same size and they shared them equally. Sara paid Becky and Carly $8 for her share of the cakes. How should this be money be fairly divided?

276. James and Adam decide to go to church on foot. They both set off from the same place. However, James walks half the distance and runs the other half. Adam on the other hand walks for half the time and runs half the time. They both run and walk at the same speed. Who will get to church first?

277. The Great Detective finds a man murdered at his home. The only clue was scrawled by the dying man on his calendar and reads:
1, 4, 9, 10, 11
There were four people in the house when he was murdered – Craig, Pearl, Linda and Jason. Who was the murderer?

278. What is the largest number you can get using two digits?

279. At a diner, Mr. Red, Mr. Blue, and Mr. White meet for lunch. They are wearing either a red, blue, or white shirt. Mr. Blue says: "Hey, did you notice we are all wearing different colored shirts from our names?" The man wearing the white shirt says: "Wow, Mr. Blue, that's right". Can you tell who is wearing what color shirt?

280. All students in the physics class also study mathematics. Half of those who study literature also study mathematics. Half of the students in the mathematics class study physics. Thirty students study literature and twenty study physics. Nobody who studies literature studies physics. How many students in the mathematics class study neither physics nor literature?

281. If you turn me on my side, I am everything, but if you cut me in half, I am nothing. What am I?

282. If you break me, I am immediately better and harder to break in the future. What am I?

283. What falls but never breaks and what breaks but never falls?

284. What liquid can contain the soul?

285. What digit is the most common between the number 1 to 1,000 inclusive?

286. Four cars, driving on the right-hand side of the road approach a crossroads from four different directions and stop at the junction. They can't decide who should go first and then all go together. However, there isn't a crash. Why is that?

287. Alice is walking through the forest of forgetfulness. She wants to know what day of the week it is. She stops and asks a lion and a unicorn. Now the lion lies all the time on Monday, Tuesday, and Wednesday. The unicorn always lies on Thursday, Friday and Saturday. Alice asks the lion what day it is, he says: "Well, yesterday was one of my lying days." Alice can't figure it out just from the lion's answer so she asks the unicorn and the unicorn says: "Yesterday was also one of my lying days." What day is it?

288. If $1 + 9 + 8 = 1$, what is $2 + 8 + 9 = ?$

289. A sphere has 3, a circle has 2 and a point has zero of what?

290. What correct equation can be formed using the mathematical symbols + and =, and the numbers 2, 3, 4 and 5?

291. The following numbers have something missing that is in the intervening numbers.
1, 4, 5, 6, 7, 9, 11
What is the next number in the sequence?

292. The root is at the top of the trunk and I grow over winter and die in the spring. What am I?

293. If you take the numbers 1 to 1 million and if they are arranged according to a certain criterion, 8 is the first number and 2022 is the last. What is the criterion that is used?

294. I notice that on my wall clock there is a time when the minute and hour hand are on top of each other, and precisely between the numbers 1 and 2. What time is it?

295. You are given the following four equations:
1111 = F
2222 = E
3333 = T
Using the same system what does 4444 equal?

296. Issues  issues
Issues  issues
Issues  issues
Issues  issues
Issues  issues
What sport do I play?

297. I am made with an egg, can hiss like bacon and my skin peels like an onion. I have plenty of backbone but without a leg. I can be long but still fit in a hole. What am I?

298. A man planted five rows of four trees but only planted 10 trees. How did he do this?

299. If a hen and a half lay an egg and a half in a day and a half, how many eggs will half a dozen hens lay in half a dozen days?

300. The land is white, and the seeds are black, and they grow in the mind of a reader. What am I?

# DIFFICULT RIDDLES ANSWERS

1.  *YOU DRAW A SHORTER LINE NEXT TO IT, AND IT BECOMES THE LONGER LINE.*

2.  *KNOWLEDGE*

3.  *HE FELL OFF THE BOTTOM STEP.*

4.  *THE LETTER 'E'*

5.  *ZERO*

6.  *THE WORD IS 'WRONG'.*

7.  *A FLAG*

8.  *DRY STONES*

9.  *IT WILL TAKE 198 SECONDS OR 3 MINUTES AND 18 SECONDS. ONCE THE LAST CUT IS MADE THE REMAINING ONE FOOT DOES NOT NEED TO BE CUT.*

10. *Y?*

11. *A FREEZER*

12. *A GLOVE*

13. **A PROMISE**

14. **DONUTS**

15. **100 CENTS OR $ 1**

16. **JUST ONE, WHICH IS CELEBRATED ANNUALLY**

17. **ONE AND A HALF**

18. **A BARBER**

19. **A STRAWBERRY**

20. **FLAGS**

21. **ALL OF THEM**

22. **LETTUCE**

23. **BAKING SODA**

24. **A MIRROR**

25. **IT HAS PROBLEMS**

26. **A SEE-SAW**

27. *LIGHT*

28. *TAXI DRIVERS*

29. *NINE (EIGHT SONS HAVE THE SAME SISTER, SO 8+1=9).*

30. *A SCREWDRIVER*

31. *A LADDER*

32. *SANDPAPER*

33. *ENGINE*

34. *A DOUGHNUT*

35. *BELLY BUTTON*

36. *A PARKING LOT*

37. *LEGS*

38. *A GLOVE*

39. *A PILLOW*

40. *WATER*

41. *THE EYE*

42.  *YOU ARE ON A CAROUSEL*

43.  *A RULER*

44.  *A TELEVISION*

45.  *IT SINKS*

46.  *IT IS BECAUSE THEIR AUNT IS YOUR MOTHER.*

47.  *A PALM*

48.  *EVERYTHING – BUILDINGS DON'T JUMP.*

49.  *YOUR FUTURE*

50.  *A NOSE*

51.  *THREE*

52.  *A BALLOON*

53.  *THE LETTER 'T'*

54.  *AN EASY ONE. IT IS A COIN OF COURSE.*

55.  *RAIN*

56. *FIRSTLY, YOU LIGHT UP THE TWO ENDS OF THE FIRST CANDLE. WHEN IT HAS FULLY BURNED, LIGHT UP ONE END OF THE SECOND CANDLE. THE FIRST CANDLE TAKES 30 MINUTES TO BURN OUT AND THE SECOND CANDLE WILL TAKE 60 MINUTES, WHICH IS A TOTAL OF 90 MINUTES.*

57. *THE BACK OF A CLOCK*

58. *THREE. THEY'RE ALL IN A ROW. DUCK 1 AND DUCK 2 ARE FOLLOWED BY DUCK 3. SO, DUCKS 1 AND 2 ARE IN FRONT OF DUCK 3, DUCKS 2 AND 3 ARE BEHIND DUCK 1 AND DUCK 2 IS IN THE MIDDLE.*

59. *THANKS*

60. *9.30*

61. *ALEX JONES AND JAMES SMITH ARE THEIR REAL NAMES. AS TWO OF THE STATEMENTS MUST BE FALSE ONE OF THE FIRST TWO MUST BE FALSE, AS WELL AS THE THIRD ONE.*

62. *YOU WOULD SEE THE SMOKE FIRST, THEN HEAR THE SOUND OF THE SHOT AND FINALLY SEE THE BULLET HITTING THE WATER.*

63. *HE WAS BORN IN THE SOUTHERN HEMISPHERE.*

64. *YOUR BREATH*

65. *I AM 25 YEARS OLD. IF YOU REVERSE THE NUMBER YOU GET 52 WHICH WILL BE TWICE MY AGE NEXT YEAR.*

66. *IF YOU TAKE OUT FOUR MARBLES THEN AT LEAST TWO WILL BE OF THE SAME COLOR.*

67. *THERE ARE MORE CHINESE MEN THAN JAPANESE MEN.*

68. *THERE WERE 11 PEOPLE. THE 10 WHO WERE LOOKING AT THE UNFORTUNATE MAN, AND THE MAN WHO DROPPED THE BOOK AS WELL.*

69. *NOBODY KNOWS*

70. *MERCURY IN A THERMOMETER*

71. *A MOBILE PHONE*

72. *A TREE. A FIFTH WEDDING ANNIVERSARY IS CELEBRATED WITH A WOODEN GIFT.*

73. *YOU CALL THE DOG YOU KEEP 'BOTH'.*

74. *NONE OF THEM. THE THREE DOCTORS WERE JACK'S SISTERS.*

75. NAME

76. TEN

77. JACK WON 5 GAMES SO BILL HAD TO WIN 5 TO CANCEL THAT OUT. IN THE END HE WON $ 7 SO THEY MUST HAVE PLAYED 17 GAMES.

78. A FEATHER

79. THE NEXT LETTER IS Y. THE SEQUENCE IS THE FIRST LETTERS OF SECONDS, MINUTES, HOURS, DAYS, WEEKS, MONTHS AND THEN YEARS.

80. LETTERS

81. BECAUSE IT HAS GREECE AT THE BOTTOM.

82. SIX DOZEN DOZENS IS GREATER.
SIX DOZEN DOZENS IS $6 \times 12 \times 12 = 864$
HALF A DOZEN DOZENS IS $1/2 \times 12 \times 12 = 72$

83. 5,500 DAYS IS 785 WEEKS WITH 5 DAYS LEFT OVER. THEREFORE, IF TODAY IS FRIDAY IT WILL BE A WEDNESDAY IN 5,500 DAYS TIME.

84. BRAZILIANS

85. **ENVELOPE**

86. **TRAFFIC LIGHTS**

87. **A KANGAROO**

88. **A VIOLIN**

89. **A COMB**

90. **A CLOUD**

91. **LIPS**

92. **TODAY**

93. **A HOT DOG**

94. **A BARBER**

95. **A IS D'S AUNT**

96. **JAMES' GARDEN IS TWICE AS BIG.**

97. **THE MOON**

**98.** *THE STATEMENT IS TRUE ONLY IF THE YOUNGEST SIBLING REACHES AT LEAST THE AGE THE OLDER ONE HAD WHEN THE YOUNGEST WAS BORN.*

**99.** *A COMPASS*

**100.** *A SHOE*

# FIENDISH RIDDLES ANSWERS

**101.** *Your father*

**102.** *A frisbee*

**103.** *An echo*

**104.** *An arrow*

**105.** *Light*

**106.** *Go*

**107.** *X – it is 24th in the alphabet and XX is 20 in Roman numerals.*

**108.** *Lungs*

**109.** *The same as yours, you're the bus driver.*

**110.** *An alarm clock*

**111.** *When the water is frozen*

**112.** *A full stop*

**113.** *A date*

*114.* THE DOCTOR IS THE SON'S MOTHER AND NOT THE FATHER.

*115.* THEY STARTED ON OPPOSITE BANKS.

*116.* A RULER

*117.* TEETH

*118.* THERE ARE 24 INHABITANTS. SIX OF THEM HAVE FOUR LEGS AND EIGHTEEN HAVE TWO.

*119.* THEY ARE FACING EAST. A RIGHT AND LEFT TURN ARE 90 DEGREES EACH AND AN ABOUT TURN IS 180 DEGREES. THEY HAVE THEREFORE JUST TURNED AROUND TO FACE THE OPPOSITE DIRECTION.

*120.* 1961

*121.* HE ASKED THE PRINCESS TO JOIN HIM.

*122.* A PENCIL

*123.* THE CAT RECEIVED $18 - $4.50 PER LEG.

*124.* SEVEN IS THE ONLY ONE WITH TWO SYLLABLES.

*125.* A GOOSE

*126.* A TIRE (ATTIRE)

*127.* THE TWO ENDS OF THE CHAIN ARE ATTACHED TO THE SAME NAIL AS 5 FOOT DOWN AND 5 FOOT BACK UP AGAIN EQUALS THE 10 FOOT LENGTH OF THE CHAIN.

*128.* YOUR BACK

*129.* THEY WERE HUSBAND AND WIFE

*130.* A DICTIONARY

*131.* AN ELASTIC BAND

*132.* FORTH, IT'S INCORRECTLY SPELLED. IT SHOULD BE FOURTH.

*133.* THE LETTER 'R'

*134.* WHEN EATING A WATERMELON

*135.* A SPIRAL STAIRCASE

*136.* THE BLIND MAN CAN SPEAK SO HE JUST TELLS THE ASSISTANT HE WANTS A COMB.

*137.* A NUN

*138. EYES*

*139. AN OVEN*

*140. THE WORD 'HERE'*

*141. I WAS FOR THE PROPOSAL.*

*142. IF 'EVERYTHING I TELL YOU IS A LIE', THEN THE STATEMENT IS TRUE AND A PARADOX. THE ONLY EXPLANATION IS THAT THE STATEMENT IS A LIE, AND I TELL YOU THE TRUTH SOMETIMES.*

*143. YOU DECIDE TO HIT YOUR BRAKES.*

*144. SARAH WILL BE TEN YEARS OLD IN FIVE YEARS, AND JUSTIN WILL BE FIFTEEN.*

*145. CHI – CA – GO*

*146. HE USES FOUR OF THE HALF FULL BOTTLES TO FILL TWO EMPTY BOTTLES. HE THEN HAS NINE FULL BOTTLES, THREE HALF FULL BOTTLES AND NINE EMPTY BOTTLES. EACH GUEST WILL GET THREE FULL BOTTLES, ONE HALF FULL BOTTLE AND THREE EMPTY BOTTLES.*

*147. A KEYHOLE*

*148.* *Four people can sit in five seats in 120 different variations (5 x 4 x 3 x 2 = 120).*

*149.* *COURTS. All of the others are anagrams of each other.*

*150.* *The emperor can load the elephant on to the ship and see how far the ship sinks in the water. He then takes the elephant off and puts items weighing 50 lbs or less, the weight of which he will know from his scales, and see how much weight he needs to put on the ship to depress it to a similar position as just having the elephant on.*

*151.* *The four corner posts are common to two sides. Therefore, he uses 28 x 4 sides plus the four corner posts. He needs 116 posts altogether.*

*152.* *She read the number upside down. It didn't say 98 but 86.*

*153.* *Tug of war*

*154.* *The snails crossed the finish line in this order: Paul, Laura, Ester, Tom.*

*155.* A CALENDAR

*156. 1+2+3+4+5+6+7+(8x9)*

*157.* SYLLABLES

*158. THE OLDEST BROTHER IS 19 YEARS OLD.*

*159. IF 80% SPEAK ENGLISH THEN 20% SPEAK JUST FRENCH. SIMILARLY, IF 60% SPEAK FRENCH THEN 40% SPEAK JUST ENGLISH. THEREFORE 60% SPEAK JUST ONE LANGUAGE (40% + 20%) AND 40% SPEAK BOTH LANGUAGES.*

*160. I AM FIRE.*

*161. YOU NEED 5 CATS. THEY EACH CATCH ONE EVERY 5 MINUTES. THEREFORE IN 100 MINUTES THEY WILL EACH CATCH 20 MICE.*

*162. THEY ARE TELLING YOU HOW CLEVER YOU ARE FOR SOLVING THE PUZZLE:*
*"TOO WISE YOU ARE, TOO WISE YOU BE, I SEE YOU ARE TOO WISE FOR ME."*

*163. HE IS 180 CENTIMETERS TALL.*

**164.** ONE QUARTER OF THE BRICK WEIGHS 3/4 OF A POUND. THEREFORE, THE WHOLE BRICK WOULD WEIGH **(3⁄4 X 4)**, WHICH IS 3 POUNDS.

**165.** THE WORD IS 'EMPTY'.

**166.** THE QUESTION YOU COULD ASK ONE OF THE SISTERS IS: IF I WERE TO ASK YOUR SISTER WHETHER YOU ALWAYS TELL THE TRUTH, WHAT WOULD SHE SAY?
IF THE REPLY IS "NO" MEANS YOU ARE TALKING TO THE TRUTH TELLER, A REPLY OF "YES" MEANS YOU ARE TALKING TO THE LIAR.

**167.** HE WILL HAVE 25 COCONUTS WITH HIM AT THE END. THE FIRST 10 CHECKPOINTS WILL REQUIRE 3 COCONUTS EACH, WHICH EMPTIES HIS FIRST SACK. THE NEXT 15 CHECKPOINTS REQUIRE 2 COCONUTS EACH, WHICH WILL EMPTY HIS SECOND STACK. NOW, HE IS LEFT WITH 1 SACK AND 5 MORE CHECKPOINTS. SO, THE 5 CHECKPOINTS WILL TAKE 1 COCONUT EACH. THEREFORE, HE WILL BE LEFT WITH 25 COCONUTS.

**168.** TIME

**169.** THE WIND

*170.* *The fifth child's name is Frank as they follow the first letter of the days of the week.*

*171.* *The Empire State Building is 443 meters high. Therefore, we would get 443 piles of pennies 1 meter high.*
*Pennies are 2 cm wide so you will get 50 per meter or 2,500 per square meter. Therefore, you will easily get the 443 piles of coins into the space.*

*172.* *In an hour the combined distance traveled will be 100 miles.*

*173.* *The train has to travel two miles to pass completely through the tunnel.*
*After starting to enter the tunnel the train would travel one mile to be completely in the tunnel. As the train is a mile-long it will need to travel another mile to be out of the tunnel. As it is traveling at 60mph and has to go 2 miles it will take two minutes.*

*174. A window*

*175. A crown*

**176.** THE RIVER WAS FROZEN

**177.** FINGERNAILS

**178.** IF YOU READ THE NUMBERS UPSIDE DOWN YOU WILL SEE THAT IT READS 'BILL IS THE BOSS HE SELLS OIL'.

**179.** A GOLF BALL

**180.** IF WE SAY THAT J IS JACK'S AGE AND F IS HIS FATHER'S AGE THEN WE KNOW:

$3J = F$

$2J = F + 11$

IF WE SOLVE THESE SIMULTANEOUS EQUATIONS WE FIND THAT JACK'S AGE IS 11 AND HIS FATHER IS 33 YEARS OLD.

**181.** THE FIVE VOWELS

**182.** RUST

**183.** WHAT TIME IS IT?

**184.** A THUMB

**185.** A SPIDER

**186.** WHEELS

**187.** A RAILROAD

**188.** LIQUID

**189.** A DECIDUOUS TREE

**190.** BLOOD

**191.** A WAVE

**192.** A MICROWAVE

**193.** A POSTMAN

**194.** MERCURY

**195.** ELECTRICITY

**196.** WITH BET A) HIS RETURN IS 50%, WITH BET B) HIS RETURN IS ABOUT 56% AND BET C) GIVES ABOUT A 42% CHANCE OF WINNING. THEREFORE, BET B) WOULD BE THE LOGICAL BET TO DOUBLE HIS MONEY.

**197.** BREAD

**198.** A LAP

**199.** THE DONKEY IS MOVING IN A CIRCULAR PATH AND HENCE THE OUTSIDE LEGS TRAVEL MORE DISTANCE THAN THE INNER LEGS.

**200.** 6

# EVIL RIDDLES ANSWERS

**201.** *A DIE (DICE)*

**202.** *HE MADE A LOSS OF $ 500. THE TWO CARS MUST HAVE BEEN BOUGHT FOR $ 5000 AND $ 7500 IF THERE IS TO BE A 20% PROFIT AND LOSS ON EACH. THIS MEANS HE PAID $ 12,500 FOR THE TWO CARS AND SOLD THEM FOR $ 12,000 RESULTING IN A $ 500 LOSS.*

**203.** *YET*

**204.** *TIME*

**205.** *IF THE FIRST STATEMENT IS CORRECT, THEN STATEMENT 2 WILL BE CORRECT AND VICE VERSA. THEREFORE, STATEMENT 3 IS THE ONLY CORRECT ONE. FROM THIS WE KNOW THAT BOX B MUST HAVE THE RED MARBLE. AS BOX C DOESN'T HAVE THE BLUE IT MUST HAVE THE WHITE, WHICH LEAVES BOX A WITH THE BLUE MARBLE.*

**206.** *A SWEATER*

**207.** *A CHAIN*

**208.** *EYE LASHES*

*209.* *It will take 15 minutes. You start with steak 1*
*and 2. After 5 minutes you turn over steak 1 and*
*take steak 2 off and put steak 3 on. After another*
*5 minutes you take steak 1 off as it is finished,*
*turn over steak 3 and put steak 2 back in the pan.*
*After another 5 minutes all three are cooked – a*
*total of 15 minutes.*

*210.* *A porcupine*

*211.* *Hi*

*212.* *Breath*

*213.* *The woman is the man's mother-in-law*

*214.* *The brothers are days of the week*

*215.* *A snail*

*216.* *A snowflake*

*217.* *The quick brown fox jumps over the lazy dog.*

*218.* *A jigsaw*

*219.* *A pacemaker*

*220.* *A* NEST

*221.* THEY ARE BOTH SURROUNDED BY WATER.

*222.* IN ROMAN NUMERALS *IV* IS FOUR AND HALF OF THAT IS *V* WHICH IS FIVE.

*223.* *A* LOCK

*224.* *A* KETTLE

*225.* *A* DOOR

*226.* THEY ARE IN ALPHABETICAL ORDER

*227.* SOPHIE

*228.* EMOJIS

*229.* TAKE THE FIRST LETTER OF EACH WORD AND PLACE IT AT THE END. *IT* WILL SPELL THE SAME WORD BACKWARDS.

*230.* THREE SISTERS AND TWO BROTHERS

*231.* ICE MELTS WITH FIRE AND FLOATS ON WATER

**232.** FRED WILL HAVE USED MORE FUEL THAN THE WEIGHT OF THE BIRD AND WILL THEREFORE BE UNDER 25 TONS.

**233.** YOU SHOULD SAY THAT YOU ARE THINKING OF NUMBER 2 OR 3 AND ASK IF THE NUMBER YOU ARE THINKING OF IS SMALLER OR EQUAL TO THE ONE THAT JACK IS THINKING OF. IF THE ANSWER IS NO THEN JACK IS THINKING OF THE NUMBER 1. IF THE ANSWER IS YES THEN JACK IS THINKING OF THE NUMBER 3.

**234.** AIR

**235.** 54223

**236.** 5 CHILDREN HAVE BARE FEET.
AS WE KNOW, 3 CHILDREN ARE WEARING BOTH. SO, ONLY 3 CHILDREN ARE WEARING ONLY SOCKS (6 – 3 = 3), AND 1 IS WEARING ONLY SHOES (4 – 3 = 1).
SO, IN TOTAL, 3 + 3 + 1 = 7. NOW, 12 CHILDREN ARE THERE, SO, 12 – 7 = 5.

**237.** THE DINNER LASTED 2 HOURS. IN 2 HOURS, THE THICK CANDLE WAS 2/3 OF THE ORIGINAL LENGTH AND THE THIN CANDLE WAS 1/3 OF THE ORIGINAL LENGTH.

**238.** *If Uncle Jack did it then 4 of the statements are true. If Aunt Mary did it then only 2 are true. If Cousin Stewart did it then 4 are true. If Uncle Jim did it then 4 are true again. However, if Cousin Margaret did it then three statements are true so she did it*

**239.** *False. Some alphas may be deltas, but it is not definite.*

**240.** *Twelve apples*

**241.** *If 20 play both sports, then 35 (55 – 20) play just basketball and 24 (44 – 20) play just baseball. Therefore, 35 + 24 + 20 = 79 and 21 play neither (100 – 79).*

**242.** *The answer must be yes (A). If Betty is married, she is looking at Bill. If she is unmarried then John is looking at her.*

**243.** *A choice*

**244.** *Sara is Julie's daughter.*

**245.** *The number is 042.*

*Based on a) and b), we can say that 6 is not the correct number.*

*Now we know that the number does not contain 6 and based on c), we know that 2 and 0 are correct numbers but in the wrong position. From a), 2's position should be on the right. The number is ??2. Based on e), 0's position should be on the left. The code is 0?2.*

*We have to find the missing number in the middle position. Based on b), the middle number has to be 4. It cannot be 1, as the statement says that the number is wrongly placed.*

**246.** *The three errors are:*
   *A) They – it should say there*
   *B) Erors should be errors*
   *C) The question asks for three errors but there are only two.*

**247.** *A clock*

**248.** *Typewriter*

**249.** *An egg*

*250. A* BEEHIVE

*251. A* MUSICIAN

*252. J*

*253. YOUR EYES*

*254. WHEN IT REACHES THE BOTTOM*

*255. WATER*

*256. A* MIRROR

*257. THERE ARE 99 RUNNERS IN THE RACE. IF HE IS THE
FIFTIETH FASTEST IN THE RACE, HE IS NUMBER 50.
HOWEVER, FOR HIM TO BE FIFTIETH SLOWEST AND
NUMBER 50 THERE MUST BE 99 RUNNERS IN THE RACE.
THERE ARE 50 NUMBERS BETWEEN 50 AND 99
INCLUSIVE.*

*258. A* BATTERY

*259. 1* AND *9*

*260. A* LIGHT SWITCH

*261. The next letters in the series are ITS. They are the initial letters of the question.*

*262. You post the box to your friend with the box locked. Your friend then puts his own lock on the box and posts it back. You take your lock off and return it to the friend. He can then open the box with his own key.*

*263. The trick here is that apples can at a minimum mean two apples. Therefore, if the tree had two apples and one blew off there wouldn't be 'apples' on the tree or the floor.*

*264. Back. The rest make a word when spelled backwards.*

*265. If you guessed three balls correctly then you will have guessed all four as it is impossible to guess just three. Therefore, as we know that 66 got none right, 42 got one right and 28 got two right that leaves just 14 from the 150 who participated. They must have got all four right.*

*266. A book*

267. *It is certain. As some people have less than 2 legs, and very few have more than 2, the average will be less than 2.*

268. *The King died because the poison was in the ice and he drank slowly enough for the ice to melt.*

269. *There were only 5 animals going to the river – the cheetah, two monkeys and two parrots. The elephants weren't going, and they all saw the same two monkeys.*

270. *The prince put 9 scorpions in each of 3 cages. Then he got a large cage and put the three smaller cages into that, thus achieving an odd number of scorpions in each cage.*

271. *He buys:*
    *80 goose eggs at a cost of 4 cents*
    *19 chicken eggs at a cost of 95 cents*
    *1 duck egg at a cost of 1 cent*
    *Totaling 100 eggs at 100 cents*

272. *You cut all four tablets in half and take half of each tablet on each day.*

**273.** *Harry's PIN is 65292.*

*The third digit in the PIN is three less than the second, and the fourth number digit is four larger than the second. Therefore, there can only be three possible combinations of the second, third and fourth digit. They are 307, 418 and 529. We also know the first digit is three times the fifth one. This means they can only be one of 3 & 1, 6 & 2 or 9 & 3. The other criterion is that three combinations of the digits also add up to 11. There is only one number that fits these criteria.*

**274.** *The tree will take 198 days to reach 100 feet.*

*On the first day it will increase by a half, which is half a foot. On the second day it will be one and a half feet and increase by a third, which is half a foot again. The tree will continue to grow by half a foot a day. Therefore in 198 days it will have grown by 99 feet, which when added to the original one foot will be 100 feet high.*

*275.* Becky, who had three cakes should get $ 1 and Carly, who had five cakes, should get $ 7. There are 8 cakes and each of the women will have eaten two and two thirds of a cake each. Therefore, Becky brought 3 cakes and Carly five and both ate two and two thirds. This means that Becky gave Sara one third of a cake and Carly gave her two and one third. This means that Carly gave 7 times as much cake to Sara as Becky and received 7 times as much money.

*276. ADAM WILL REACH THE DESTINATION FIRST.*

*SUPPOSE THE DISTANCE TO THE CHURCH IS 12 MILES AND
THEY BOTH WALK AT A RATE OF 2 MILES PER HOUR AND
RUN AT A RATE OF 6 MILES PER HOUR. USE THE FORMULA:
RT = D (RATE X TIME = DISTANCE) TO FIND EACH
PERSON'S TIME.*

*JAMES WHO WALKS HALF THE DISTANCE AND RUNS HALF
THE DISTANCE:*

*2T = 6 MILES, SO T = 3 HOURS WALKING*

*6T = 6 MILES, SO T = 1 HOUR RUNNING*

*T = 4 HOURS TOTAL TIME*

*ADAM WHO WALKS HALF THE TIME AND RUNS HALF THE
TIME:*

*2(0.5T) + 6(0.5T) = 12 MILES*

*T + 3T = 12*

*4T = 12*

*T = 3 HOURS TOTAL TIME*

*THEREFORE, ADAM GETS TO THE CHURCH FIRST.*

*277. THE MURDERER WAS JASON. THE NUMBERS ARE THE 1ST
LETTERS OF THE MONTHS OF THE YEAR ON THE CALENDAR.
THE FIRST MONTH IS JANUARY, THE 4TH APRIL ETC.*

*278. $9^9 = 387420489$*

**279.** *Blue could only be wearing white or red and we know that there is already someone else wearing the white shirt so Mr. Blue could only be wearing the red shirt. Mr. White could have only been wearing a blue or a red shirt, and red is already taken, so Mr. White is wearing a blue shirt. Mr. Red now has to be wearing a white shirt.*

**280.** *We know that 20 students study physics, and half the students in the mathematics class study physics. That means that there are 40 students in the mathematics class. We also know that there are 30 who study literature and half of these study mathematics. Therefore 15 study literature and mathematics. As none do physics and literature we know that 20 do physics and mathematics and 15 do literature and mathematics. Therefore, out of 40 mathematical students 35 take an additional option and 5 do just mathematics.*

**281.** *The number 8*

**282.** *A record*

**283.** *Day and night*

**284.** INK

**285.** THE NUMBER **1** IS THE MOST COMMON. IT HAS **301** OCCURRENCES COMPARED TO **300** OF THE OTHER NUMBERS. THE ONLY REASON IS BECAUSE THE NUMBER **1,000** IS INCLUDED.

**286.** THEY ALL TURN RIGHT

**287.** TODAY IS THURSDAY. IF WHAT THE LION SAYS IS TRUE THEN IT MUST BE A THURSDAY, AND IF WHAT THE UNICORN SAYS IS TRUE THEN IT MUST BE SUNDAY. HOWEVER, ON SUNDAY THEY BOTH TELL THE TRUTH SO IT CAN'T BE SUNDAY AND THE LION IS TELLING THE TRUTH.

**288.** THE ANSWER IS TEN. IF YOU TAKE THE FIRST LETTER OF THE EQUATION YOU GET THE ANSWER:
ONE + NINE + EIGHT = ONE
TWO + EIGHT + NINE = TEN

**289.** DIMENSIONS

**290.** $3^2 = 4 + 5$

**291.** THEY ARE MISSING THE LETTER 'T'. THE NEXT NUMBER AFTER **11** WHICH DOES NOT HAVE A 'T' IS **100**.

*292. An icicle*

*293. The numbers are arranged alphabetically.*

*294. 12.00. The hands are precisely between the 1 and
2 of 12.*

*295. 1111 = Four*
   *2222 = Eight*
   *3333 = Twelve*
   *4444 = Sixteen*

*296. Tennis. Ten issues = tennis shoes*

*297. A snake*

*298. He planted the trees in the pattern of a 5-pointed
star with a tree at each intersection.*

**299.** *The trick is to find the daily rate of egg laying.*

*Hens x days x (daily rate) = eggs*

*1.5 x 1.5 x (daily rate) = 1.5*

*Daily rate = 1.5/1.5 x 1.5*

*Daily rate = 2/3*

*So, 1 hen in 1 day will lay 2/3 of an egg*

*Therefore 6 hens in 6 days will lay:*

*6 x 6 x 2/3 = 24*


**300.** *A book*

# ONE LAST THING

If you have enjoyed this book, I would love you to write a review of it on Amazon. It is really useful feedback as well as untold encouragement to the author.

Any remarks are highly appreciated, so if you have any comments, or suggestions for improvements to this publication, or for other books, I would love to hear from you.

You can contact me at
*m.prefontaine2@gmail.com*

All your input is greatly valued, and the books have already been revised and improved as a result of helpful suggestions from readers.

Thank you.

Made in the USA
Middletown, DE
18 December 2020

29076147R00057